RESTORED & Remarried

Workbook

RESTORED & Remarried

ENCOURAGEMENT FOR REMARRIED COUPLES IN A STEPFAMILY

Workbook

Seven Trees
Media

GIL & BRENDA STUART

A Publication of Seven Trees Media
Vancouver, WA | USA 360-904-2117 | www.seventreesmedia.com

Cover art by Katie Bredemeier.
Design and layout by Michelle DeMonnin, DeMonnin's Art Studio, Inc.
for Burck Communications, www.burckcommunications.com
Photo of Gil and Brenda Stuart by Niccole W Photography, Vancouver, WA

ISBN: 978-0-557-10869-5

Contents

Introduction

Restored & Remaried — An Interactive Seminar and Workbook for Remarried Couples in a Stepfamily

You never forget the train wreck of divorce, the scene of the courtroom, the hours of loneliness, or the questions of "Why?" with no answers. Or perhaps you've lost a spouse to death, and the world you built has vanished in tragedy or long months of painful decline.

Whichever may be your experience, you keep breathing and making it through another day. Months or years may pass until your heart is ready to love again. Although you're hesitant at first, memories or shame (you may feel from past failures) keep you from a fulfilling future of companionship with trust and honesty as the foundation.

We are stating obvious points around the remarried experience, but also have a willingness to step forward and say it out loud. We are presenting concepts and terms that a person who may be in his or her second or multiple marriage relationship can readily grasp, because the second time around has a bundle of issues unique to themselves. Can you relate?

God in His wisdom created the relationship we call marriage. We are on this adventure with you. As we study, read, discuss, and chew on the issue of marriage, we'll open up our hearts to God's way when it is the next time around. The Book states that marriage is for life. We are not condoning loopholes about remarriage here, but sharing provisions in the Book for any of us that mess up the rules or have someone (ex-spouse) ditch and run.

With that said, let's get started! We presume that those of you who are using these materials are either remarried, considering the idea of such an adventure, or have been at the process awhile. As you head into the material, keep this one thought in mind...

> *"If you ain't got the marriage you ain't got nothin'!"*

Respectfully – "Restored & Remarried"

Gil and Brenda Stuart

Gil and Brenda Stuart
Founding Board Members of Thriving Families of Clark County
Prepare and Enrich certified through Life Innovations
Marriage CoMission Partners

Instructions

Each session in the workbook correlates to a session in the seminar. There are eight weeks to address topics that a remarried couple/family deals with daily in some shape or form.

Workbook weekly components are:

1. Introduction to session topic

2. Scripture for reflection and discussion

3. Quote to encourage and strengthen

4. Questions for group or couple discussion

5. Acrostic – key words that become "catch words" between you

    Each week we will offer a word that we think builds a great marriage. From that word, you create an acrostic that you both contribute to that represents the marriage you want. Take a few days to think it through before you come back and share it with your spouse. Here's an example. Let's say having fun is an important part of your vibrant relationship. The acrostic would look like this:

	Hers	His
F	Free	Fabulous
U	Unique	Ultimate
N	Nutty	Nudity!

    When you come back together, you can talk about the words you came up with individually. It's exciting to see what words you have in common and what words will bring further discussion.

    We encourage you to find words that would describe what YOU, as a couple, represents a GREAT marriage.

    An acrostic can be found at the end of each chapter.

6. Add the brick to your wall (your wall is on page 77)

    Unlike the walls we build that come between us, you will build a wall that will be a type of protection for your marriage. A brick will be added each week that will represent a key concept that is part of the great marriage you want. The acrostic or "catch word" developed and agreed upon is then placed as a brick in your wall. The first three bricks have already been placed in

your wall for you: Christ and Commitment. As you find words that are important and unique to your relationship, add them to your wall! Be creative and have fun.

7. Action steps – a call to "actions" that apply from the questions

8. A closing prayer – written to encourage both of you and to pray for one dimension of your relationship

Week 1

Community

1. Intro

Welcome! Our first week together is important. This is a time for you, as a group, to get to know one another. Let's all get on the same page! Relax and enjoy!

The reason remarriages can fail so easily is because of the lack of two components: resources and fellowship/community. By participating in the "Restored & Remarried" study, you are taking the steps to protect and strengthen your marriage. We applaud you!

In our fast-paced world, building trust and honesty in a community setting with people you barely know is a high expectation of anyone. You may be sharing about some of the most painful periods of your life, but also the most exciting chapters that lie ahead.

Let's build some strong allies to travel with you into the new stuff – the hopes and dreams that lie ahead can be better when shared. Others who have experienced similar hardships can relate more quickly and at the gut level, therefore making the risk of reaching out all worthwhile.

Leaning on one another is not a sign of weakness! It is evidence you have learned to reach out as well as being confident to ask for counsel. Share your experiences because you never know who will benefit or be saved the heartache of what you learned the hard way. Now that is community and working together! Plus it can be fun!

2. Verse

Philippians 2:1-2

"Therefore if there is any encouragement in Christ, if there is any consolation of love, if there is any fellowship of the Spirit, if any affection and compassion, make my joy complete by being of the same mind, maintaining the same love, united in spirit, intent on one purpose."

3. Quote

Herman Melville

"We cannot live only for ourselves. A thousand fibers connect us with our fellow men."

4. Questions

Questions to ponder before your first week and to discuss as a group:

1. How are we doing as a couple?

   _____

   _____

   _____

   _____

   _____

   _____

2. How are we doing as a family?

   _____

   _____

   _____

   _____

   _____

   _____

   _____

3. What are our strengths?

_____

_____

_____

_____

_____

_____

4. What are our weaknesses?

_____

_____

_____

_____

_____

_____

5. What does community look like to us?

_____

_____

_____

_____

_____

_____

Definition of community can be different for everyone. It can mean a place to:

Be encouraged

Share (not a gripe session)

Get a different viewpoint

Get some perspective

Build friendships

Have accountability

Live life

Have fun!

6. At the end of our study series together, what are our expectations?

_____

_____

_____

_____

_____

_____

_____

5. Acrostic (his and hers)

We'll start this next week.

6. Add the acrostic as a brick in your wall

We'll start this next week.

7. Action steps

1. Pray for the families represented in your new group.

2. Do your homework.

3. Make a list of some positive words that describe your marriage.

_____

_____

_____

_____

_____

_____

_____

4. Make time to share your positive words with each other!

8. Closing prayer

Lord, thank You for my spouse. We ask that You lead us through the next seven weeks of our time in this workbook. Open our hearts to each other, and to You. Give us courage to be sensitive to what You need to say to us and for us to respond. Lord, thank You for our family. At times things seem so hard and confusing. Show us how to be understanding of all of our family members and help us experience Your grace. Remind us to laugh, too!

Week 2

Restored Foundations

1. Intro

Have you ever felt like a second-class Christian because you're part of a stepfamily? That's IMPOSSIBLE because there is no such thing as a first-class Christian. At the foot of the cross the ground is level and all are welcome. There is no shame. No second places.

A startling comment we heard recently was that a couple does not have to have God in their marriage to have a successful marriage. God makes it easier, but we're told the DNA of relationships in great marriages is **trust and honesty**. It's all about doing the right thing. Sometimes that means to just be nice to each other!

Unfortunately, if you look around, the human race doesn't have that down too well. The hearts of men and women long for connection in their marriages and families. A first marriage can be lost due to its foundation being shaken for many reasons, but with Christ and Commitment being restored, there is hope to rebuild and strengthen the stepfamily.

Trust and honesty in our society have been reduced to "if it feels good do it." It's called situational ethics and self-gratification, and we want it right now! That's where God's biblical design makes it easier. Can you trust Him to restore you from the train wreck called divorce?

To begin rebuilding and encouraging stepfamilies, let's tackle a few myths:

- If you put unrelated people in the same house, they naturally will love and care for one another.

- The new marriage/family competes against the legacy of the previous one. (Is it fun playing the comparison game?)

- Everything will fall into place over time.

- Kids will adjust and be happy about the remarriage.

2. Verse

Haggai 2:8-9 (NIV)

"'The silver is Mine and the gold is Mine,' declares the LORD of hosts. 'The latter glory of this house will be greater than the former,' says the LORD of hosts, 'and in this place I will give peace,' declares the LORD of hosts."

Psalm 118: 6-8 (NIV)

"The LORD is with me; I will not be afraid. What can man do to me? The LORD is with me; he is my helper. I will look in triumph on my enemies. It is better to take refuge in the LORD than to trust in man."

3. Quote

Unknown

"Sorrow looks back; worry looks around; but faith looks up."

4. Questions

1. Do you feel there is a stigma about being a stepfamily or remarried? Why or why not?

_____

_____

_____

_____

_____

_____

_____

2. Give an example of when/how you may have experienced in society or church the stigma of being divorced/remarried or part of a stepfamily.

    _____

    _____

    _____

    _____

    _____

    _____

3. What myths have you fallen prey to in your remarriage/stepfamily?

    _____

    _____

    _____

    _____

    _____

    _____

    _____

4. Why do you think the divorce rate can be so high for remarried couples?

    _____

    _____

    _____

    _____

    _____

    _____

5. What does trust mean to you?

_____

_____

_____

_____

_____

_____

6. How would you explain honesty?

_____

_____

_____

_____

_____

_____

7. Why is having a strong marriage important for your family?

_____

_____

_____

_____

_____

_____

5. Acrostic (his and hers): TRUST

Safety is the mortar that holds you/us together – knowing that your honesty/trust will not be used against you and that betrayal of confidence is not an optional vice aimed at each other.

6. Add the acrostic as a brick in your wall (see pages 79)

7. Action steps

1. Celebrate your stepfamily (no matter how long you've been stepping).

2. Share your acrostic.

3. Plan a date with your spouse with these conditions:

   - No talking about kids, money, pets, in-laws, out-laws, job, or ex's! (What's left?)

   - Initiate discussion about trust and honesty.

8. Closing prayer

Heavenly Father, we come to You with surrendered hearts together before You and toward each other. Jesus, we ask that You would help us see the redemptive work of the cross in our lives. We intercede for each other and all children who are under our care. Open our eyes to really see and know that we can trust You with everything. Restore peace and grant understanding so we listen to You first as we work to rebuild our lives and enjoy the restoration You have for us together.

TRUST

To restore confidence in your relationship

	HERS	HIS
T		
R		
U		
S		
T		

"Can they offer sacrifices? Can they finish in a day? Can they revive the stones from the dusty rubble even the burned ones?"

Nehemiah 4:2b (NASB)

Can you fully trust again?

Do the Right Thing

If you have to ask,
"What is the right thing?"
you are being selfish.

Week 3

Cornerstone of Commitment

1. Intro

Keeping the mortar strong between the bricks in your wall is crucial. Prayer can be a bonding agent.

Prayer is intimate between spouses. It can be intimidating and freeing at the same time. We have talked to so many couples who do not pray together. It's hard to pray when there is something in contention or just bothersome between the two of you. You may tend to pray *at* each other instead of *for* each other or with each other.

In the majority of marriages, couples are not praying together, and men are not leading spiritually. Why is that?

If you are not praying together, we encourage you to take the first step. When you go to bed at night, just thank the Lord for the day. If morning is better, ask Him to lead you through your day together!

Did you know that marital sex is better when you pray together? Go pray....

Walls are not meant to be between spouses, but both are to come behind the wall for protection of their marriage. Christ is the sure foundation not only in marriage but also in your life. In the Old Testament, Christ is referenced as the chief cornerstone (Psalm 118:22).

With Christ and commitment as the foundation of your wall, you're reminded:

- to be dedicated to your spouse.

- there are no back doors (exits) to the relationship.

- of your commitment to making your marriage and family work.

- The D-word (divorce) is not in your vocabulary.

Remember, the fight is FOR your marriage. Don't let things – and especially the kids – come in between!

The attitude of commitment keeps you investing in your marriage and your family. Be intentional about trust and honesty, and you have the makings of a strong and healthy marriage. Remember, you don't want a good marriage…you want a great marriage!

2. Verse

Nehemiah 4:2, 6 (NIV)

"'Can they bring the stones back to life from those heaps of rubble – burned as they are?'" (verse 2). "So we rebuilt the wall till all of it reached half its height, for the people worked with all their heart" (verse 6).

(Please take time to read Nehemiah 4:1-10.)

3. Quote

Autumn Ray, Co-Founder of Marriage Team (www.MarriageTeam.org)

"OK, you're committed to your marriage. Are you committed to being unhappy and miserable, or are you willing to change?"

4. Questions

1. What did you learn from your mistake or mishap from your previous marriage/relationship?

_____

_____

_____

_____

_____

_____

2. What are the strengths you bring to your marriage?

_____

_____

_____

_____

_____

_____

3. What strengths does your spouse bring to your marriage?

_____

_____

_____

_____

_____

_____

4. On a scale of 1 to 10 (1 being the lowest), how comfortable are you praying? Why?

_____

_____

_____

_____

_____

_____

_____

5. On a scale of 1 to 10 (1 being the lowest), how comfortable are you praying together? Why?

_____

_____

_____

_____

_____

_____

_____

6. When it comes to your marriage, what things will erode your commitment? (e.g., lack of trust, honesty, selfishness)

_____

_____

_____

_____

_____

_____

_____

7. Here is a chance to really test your trust and honesty…are you ready?

- On a scale of 1 to 10 (1 being the lowest), how committed are you to your spouse?

  _____

- On a scale of 1 to 10 (1 being the lowest), how committed are you to your stepfamily?

  _____

Discuss this with your spouse. If you are not at 10, how can you improve?

_____

_____

_____

_____

_____

_____

_____

8. Describe what a wall looks like when it comes between you and your spouse.

_____

_____

_____

_____

_____

_____

_____

9. Describe what a wall looks like when it is protecting you and your spouse.

_____

_____

_____

_____

_____

_____

_____

_____

5. Acrostic (his and hers): GREAT

Share from last week TRUST.

6. Add the acrostic as a brick in your wall (see pages 79)

7. Action steps

1. Establish a prayer life. Remember that prayer:

   • Seeks God's heart for the moment or situation.

   • Agrees with God for His purposes to be fulfilled in people or situations.

   • Applies God's truths in dealing with selfishness and asking Him to change our hearts and attitudes.

2. Share your acrostic.

3. Plan a date with your spouse with these conditions:

   • No talking about kids, money, pets, in-laws, out-laws, job, or ex's!

   • Talk about prayer, your wall, and what you are committed to.

8. Closing prayer

Lord, show us what a GREAT marriage looks like for us. Jesus, we give You full and total claim to our lives as husband and wife and as a couple. We ask for strength and protection from issues that can crush us, and for Your intervention for my spouse with those things that can hinder him/her from fully trusting You and me.

Lead us into deeper truth of building commitments based in You that will sustain us in tough times right now and ahead. Speak to each of us directly about specific areas You want to heal and create safety between us. We depend on You; lead us most Holy One.

GREAT

	HERS	HIS
G		
R		
E		
A		
T		

"Do not call to mind former things, or ponder things of the past. Behold, I will do something new, now it will spring forth; will you not be aware of it?"

Isaiah 42:9 (NASB)

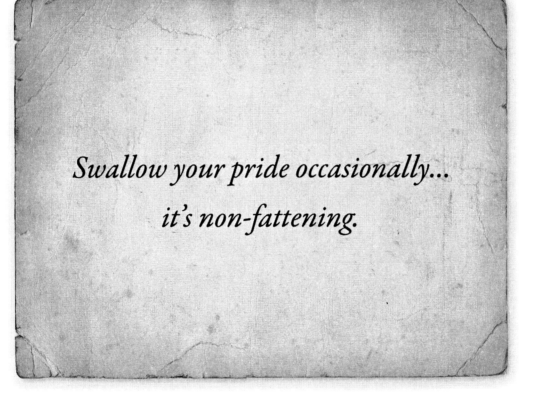

Swallow your pride occasionally...

it's non-fattening.

Week 4

"I Didn't Think It Was Going to Be Like This"

Catch Words (Part 1)

1. Intro

Do you have a language between you and your spouse – special words or phrases that are only for each other's ears? (No, we're not talking about pet names like honey bun, smoochey face, or sweet cheeks.) A unique language builds intimacy as well as strengthens your communication. Plus, it's fun.

Living the blended family adventure covers a lot of new territory in which there can be confusion and conflict. That's because you find it difficult to define what you are experiencing – physically, emotionally, or spiritually.

We created useful catch words to unravel thoughts and feelings that were overwhelming and possibly destructive to the wall protecting our marriage and family. Think through what catch words you may have. The goal is to create your own catch words that will be useful when you encounter confusion and conflict.

Those of you who have attended the Restored and Remarried seminar may have done some of this work already. Take this time to revisit and expand on what you first discussed. If this is all new to you, the following are words/phrases with which to work.

Open Door (mental connection to the past)

- This can be the process of exposing difficult circumstances from the past that shut you down.

- You hesitate to open up because of a variety of reasons: sharing tough stuff is uncomfortable, and it may still hurt.

- You have to be able to trust, be patient and sensitive; it takes time.

- You have to be willing to open the door; you choose to open it.

How will she know if you don't tell her?

Are you giving your man a safe place to share?

Bare Wire (emotional connection to the past)

- A word or statement from your spouse that sets off a painful emotional trigger from your past that you may not have even been aware of.

- Accidentally found or exposed.

- This has nothing to do with your spouse; it has to do with you.

- Acknowledgment of the bare wire to your spouse allows healing. Let Christ be your electrical tape to bring restoration and healing.

They don't know they don't know.

Sneaker Wave (situational connections to the past)

- The power of the emotion/wave is from the past (usually a situation).

- They come out of the blue; you don't see it coming.

- They can knock you off your feet.

- You need to SURF it together!

- Your spouse realizes it's something you are dealing with (from your past) and it's not the spouse's fault.

It's not about them, it's all about you!

2. Verse

James 5:16 (AMPLIFIED BIBLE)

"Confess to one another therefore your faults (your slips, your false steps, your offenses, your sins) and pray [also] for one another, that you may be healed and restored [to a spiritual tone of mind and heart]. The earnest (heartfelt, continued) prayer of a righteous man makes tremendous power available [dynamic in its working]."

3. Quote

Unknown

"A successful marriage requires falling in love many times...always with the same person."

4. Questions

1. On a scale of 1 to 10 (1 being the lowest), how safe do you feel sharing with your spouse? Why?

_____

_____

_____

_____

_____

_____

_____

2. What would discourage you from opening a door? How can your spouse help?

_____

_____

_____

_____

_____

_____

_____

3. What is a Bare Wire that gets easily hit? How do you react?

_____

_____

_____

_____

_____

_____

4. What words would describe how you would feel to share an Open Door or a Bare Wire (e.g., scared, embarrassed, encouraged, really want to but…)?

_____

_____

_____

_____

_____

_____

_____

5. Share a situation that happened that you can now label as a Sneaker Wave.

_____

_____

_____

_____

_____

_____

_____

6. How can your spouse SURF this wave with you? (e.g., you need space, you need to talk, they just need to listen, you need help fixing it)

_____

_____

_____

_____

_____

_____

_____

5. Acrostic (his and hers): HONESTY

Share from last week GREAT.

6. Add the acrostic as a brick in your wall (see pages 79)

7. Action steps

1. Decide what it is going to take between the two of you to have these catch words be applied (e.g., what does it mean to you to have a safe place to share?).

2. OK, now you can talk about it! Come up with a new pet name for each other this week. Have fun with this.

3. Share your acrostic.

4. Plan a date with your spouse with these conditions:

   • No talking about kids, money, pets, in-laws, out-laws, job, or ex's!

   • Ask what meaningful acts show love in little ways to each other (e.g.: guys, make the bed when she least expcets it; girls, welcome your man home with a big hug and kiss every night this week). What is special to you?

8. Closing prayer

In quietness and meditation, Lord Jesus, we call upon You to instruct us to love as You love us. We have wounds and misunderstandings we do not understand ourselves. We confess that we need Your help and insight to release us from bondage that keeps us trapped. Father God, creator of human emotion, we rely upon You to correct our thinking to align with Your truth. Your truth is that if we surrender to Your words of truth, You can change our hearts, which will change the way we live and love!

HONESTY

Deepens and reinforces your relationship

	HERS	HIS
H		
O		
N		
E		
S		
T		
Y		

*"Repay no one evil for evil, but take thought for what
is honest and proper and noble [aiming to be above
reproach] in the sight of everyone."*

Romans 12:17 (AMPLIFIED BIBLE)

"The key to a good marriage
is the same as the key to
living in California.
When you find a fault
don't dwell on it."

Week 5

"I Didn't See This Coming"

Catch Words (Part 2)

1. Intro

Continuing from last week, we'd like to introduce four more catch words to bolster your communication. Remember, this is a unique language to build intimacy as well as a fun activity. We want to emphasize that these catch words are useful to unravel confusion and conflict in daily interactions. Having clear communication will save many hours of needless fighting and lots of money on counselors!

Catch words:

- bring depth to your relationship

- bring intrigue

- develop your history as a couple

- keep the allure alive

- make the present richer to your relationship

Those of you who have attended the Restored and Remarried seminar may have done some of this work already. Take this time to revisit and expand on what you first discussed. If this is all new to you, the following are words/phrases with which to work.

Old Tapes/New Tapes

- Old ways of how things used to be done or perceived to be true.

- Negative habits and patterns you call yourself on as old destructive behaviors.

- Identify these old habits and patterns, then reprogram and replace.

- If you are struggling with reprogramming, don't hesitate to ask for help from your spouse or close friends.

We're not playing Old Tapes anymore!

We're doing DVDs!

Foxhole

Foxhole: a pit dug hastily for individual cover from attack. Foxholes are dark, sometimes muddy, not comfortable.

- situation or circumstance that is difficult

- emotionally and relationally charged (kids, ex's, job)

- hurtful, remorseful, bloody, scary

The response is to dig in the Foxhole and ride it out.

- hunkering down, out of the line of fire

- you're not going anywhere

- you have each other's back

This can be a strengthening point for a couple. It's an opportunity to grow stronger by protecting each other during the encounter/battle, whatever the situation is.

Watch each other's back. The Lord is in there, too!

Phantoms

For the sake of definition, Phantoms/Ghosts can be:

- photos

- memorabilia

- keepsakes

- trinkets, material objects that stimulate emotions connected to the past

Like a wisp of air, these uncanny gut punches are gone as fast as they came.

These random tangible material objects quicken the memory and can trigger either positive or negative feelings in both of you. Mysteriously, your response could be remorse, apprehension, feeling left out, or oddly warmhearted at the same time.

Short Accounts

- Short Accounts are in the here and now.

- Do not allow "stuff" (gripes, complaints, suggestions) to pile up; it can and will blow up at the worst possible time.

- It's best to safely, tenderly deal with the issue as soon as possible.

- Take it to the Lord first, before your spouse.

It's the little things that destroy a relationship.

It's the little things that make a relationship.

2. Verse

James 1:19-20 (NASB)

"This you know, my beloved brethren. But everyone must be quick to hear, slow to speak and slow to anger; for the anger of man does not achieve the righteousness of God."

3. Quote

Oscar Eliason

"Break your bad habits forever! God specializes in things thought impossible."

4. Questions

1. Identify an Old Tape (having to do with ex-spouse, kids, self-image). Write it out:

_____

_____

_____

_____

_____

_____

_____

Reprogram the above Old Tape into a new DVD. Write it below:

_____

_____

_____

_____

_____

_____

_____

2. When a conflict or discussion arises, what Old Tape do you revert to from your previous marriage/relationship?

_____

_____

_____

_____

_____

_____

_____

3. What recent Foxhole have you experienced? Did you feel as if you were in it alone? What can you do differently when the next Foxhole comes along (because it will)?

_____

_____

_____

_____

_____

_____

4. Share any experiences with Phantoms that you have encountered.

_____

_____

_____

_____

_____

_____

5. Why do couples have a problem keeping Short Accounts?

_____

_____

_____

_____

_____

_____

_____

6. What current Short Account needs to be cleared with your spouse?

_____

_____

_____

_____

_____

_____

_____

5. Acrostic (his and hers): TALK

Share from last week HONESTY.

6. Add the acrostic as a brick in your wall (see pages 79)

7. Action steps

1. Agree upon a time frame that you will allow unresolved Short Accounts to be discussed and cleared: daily, weekly, monthly? (Don't wait too long!)

2. What do you need from each other while in a Foxhole experience (e.g., just listen, talk me through it, hold me, pray, brainstorm together in how to fix it)?

3. Share your acrostic.

4. Plan a date with your spouse with these conditions:

   • No talking about kids, money, pets, in-laws, out-laws, job, or ex's!

   • Choose one of your favorite recreational activities and go have fun! How about: ice skating, bowling, watch a ball game, putt-putt golf, hike, or a walk?

8. Closing prayer

Christ Jesus, Your Word says that when we accept and surrender to You, old things pass away and all things become new. Today, we ask for reconciliation of our hearts and emotions from the past, whether it was a hurt that we brought upon ourselves or someone else's trespass against us.

We ask for wisdom as to how to stand together in wisdom and grace for the protection of our marriage. No matter the issue, Lord Jesus, help us to turn to You first and abide in You rather than get pulled away in distress. We choose to rest in You!

Give us the mercy to be quick to forgive and look to You to teach us deeper truths from Your Word for each life situation.

TALK

Listening is part of talking

	HERS	HIS
T		
A		
L		
K		

"This you know, my beloved brethren. But everyone must be quick to hear, slow to speak and slow to anger; for the anger of man does not achieve the righteousness of God."

James 1:19-20 (NASB)

Husbands,

cherish your wives.

Wives,

admire your husbands

...and tell them.

Week 6

Those People *(Part 1)*

1. Intro

It's time to talk about our kids. We lovingly refer to them as THOSE PEOPLE. What are THOSE PEOPLE doing; when are THOSE PEOPLE leaving? We're going to talk about your THOSE PEOPLE in this session (if you have THOSE PEOPLE, in or out of your home). The following are realities and explanations of situations regarding THOSE PEOPLE and how they affect your marriage.

- Blending style

  Are you a blender where everyone is squished; a microwave where everyone is rushed; or a crockpot where you let each child be himself/herself and not force them into roles you see for them?

- Discipline = Time and relationship/foundation built

  Discipline flows from relationship and responsibility. Respect and building history allows you to speak into the child's life, whether he is 2 or 25.

- Rocks in bucket

  Picture your kids carrying a bucket back and forth from your ex's home to yours. Are you putting positive things in the bucket that are not a burden for them? A rock (burden) would sound like this: "Have your mom buy those shoes for you. I give her support money." (The bucket represents the container of the child's well being. Comments are the rocks that weigh down what your child carries around.)

- Strings = Manipulation

  "Why would you want to go to your dad's house after the dance when you can have your friends here to watch a movie on our new 52-inch screen TV?"

- Put yourself in your kids' shoes. They did not ask for the divorce/death. Some may have benefited from a new mom/dad, but most kids did not ask for a new mom/dad figure.

- Time frame for acceptance

  Generally speaking, whatever the age the child is when you are married, that is how long it will take for your child to accept the new stepparent. If the child is 11, for example, when you remarry, anticipate 11 years for that child to accept the stepparent as a parental figure. Adult children may never accept you as a parental figure; however, it really depends upon the circumstances. When in doubt, respect their position and love them!

- Have you grieved the loss of your previous family? Have you allowed your kids to experience the process? Allowing yourself and your kids to grieve will bring strength to the family. We underestimate the power of unresolved grief. It can come out as fear, anger, depression, and rebellion. You may need to protect each other through this process. Remember, you are a team!

  Grief takes time. It is a process of letting go of something familiar and taking hold of something in the future. Don't ever say, "You shouldn't feel that way." Listen to their concerns. God cares about how we handle our circumstances.

- We recognize that at times we are not laughing enough. How about you?

  Humor does indeed reduce friction. Did you know that a giggle is good for you in these ways: It stops you from getting sick, and it burns calories. In fact, doctors say a 15-minute laughing session burns off 40 calories. If you did this every day, you'd lose 4 pounds a year! Laughter stops stress and keeps your heart healthy.

2. Verse

Proverbs 17:22 (NASB)

"A joyful heart is good medicine."

3. Quote

Ben Franklin

"Before marriage keep both eyes open; after marriage keep one eye shut."

4. Questions

1. What is your blending style (blender, microwave, or a crockpot)? How's that working?

    _____

    _____

    _____

    _____

    _____

    _____

    _____

2. What is your discipline style? Has it been built on relationship and respect, or have you been demanding? How can you improve?

    _____

    _____

    _____

    _____

    _____

    _____

    _____

3. What rocks have you put in your kids' buckets lately? Is an apology needed?

    _____

    _____

    _____

    _____

    _____

    _____

4. Put trust and honesty to the test. Ask your kids where they are hurting. Listen, do not criticize, and make it safe for them. Do it with your spouse. This gives the stepparent an opportunity to hear the heart of the child. Do you have reservations about attempting this? Pray before you do it.

_____

_____

_____

_____

_____

_____

_____

5. How have you let your child(ren) grieve the loss of their previous family? The bigger question is…how have you?

_____

_____

_____

_____

_____

_____

_____

6. Finding comic relief in a stepfamily enhances flexibility and reduces stress. What has been one of the funniest stories in your stepfamily you can laugh about?

_____

_____

_____

_____

_____

_____

5. Acrostic (his and hers): LAUGH

Share from last week TALK

6. Add the acrostic as a brick in your wall (see pages 79)

7. Action steps

1. Share your acrostic.

2. Plan a date with your bio kids.

3. Plan a date with your stepkids.

4. List three positive qualities in each of your kids in your family (bio and step; in or out of the home).

_____

_____

_____

_____

_____

_____

_____

_____

_____

_____

_____

_____

8. Closing prayer

Children are a blessing from You, Lord...all children, even my new children, Lord, are a blessing. Yes, they offer me new challenges to grow and love and learn and deepen my trust in You! Jesus, I give You my children and the joy and frustrations that they may bring. Most importantly, Jesus, I give these kids to You to love and heal. They are hurting and confused and hiding due to a confusing mixed-up world; bring peace to them.

LAUGH

Are we laughing enough?

	HERS	HIS
L		
A		
U		
G		
H		

"A joyful heart is good medicine."

Proverbs 17:22 (NASB)

Focus

on what

is

working.

Week 7

Those People *(Part 2)*

1. Intro

The structure of a blended family has not only changed but also been rearranged.

According to Ron Deal, "It's easy for the marriage to get lost in the stepfamily forest."

In this lesson we will focus on co-parenting, the parent team, and the extended family.

A natural connection between the bio parents because of the child is unavoidable. Close off all old emotions to your child's bioparent so they don't affect the co-parenting process. Are there still emotional strings – perhaps guilt or anger – connecting you? Have you emotionally cut and cauterized your relationship with your child's bio parent? If you haven't, this will directly impact your new marriage. When co-parenting, it's all about the kids, it's not about you.

Identify what type of co-parenting relationship you have with the other bio parent. Are you: Perfect Pals, Cooperative Colleagues, Angry Associates, Fiery Foes, or Dissolved Duos? Is this working for you? Does it need to be adjusted or changed? Remember, your kids are traveling from two different countries; they are citizens of two different lands. When it is time for your kids to go back to the other home, is it pleasant for them or like a POW swap? Do not put the kids in the middle as a messenger, spy, or peacemaker no matter what their age. This is all about maintaining their well being. It's important to keep schedules the same for the kids for consistency, security, and stability. Have clear expectations with your children about your house rules, especially if they differ from the other home.

Changing birth orders needs to be recognized and talked through in a positive way. You still need to be a united front, a parental team just as you would if you were in a nuclear family. Discuss issues or difficult circumstances behind closed doors before addressing the child or the family. Family meetings should be fun, but "pink elephants" (stinky situations) do occur. Pink elephants can be scary or uncomfortable circumstances that we want to ignore. But growth and healing can be the result of working through the issue. Our tough conversations are introduced by saying, "We need to talk about a pink elephant." Our kids then know what we mean.

What about relatives who were on the outside of your train wreck looking in? There can be a sense of loss for them, too. We shouldn't ignore the extended family. Unresolved hurt or grieving may need to be addressed. We need to support positive relationships our kids have with extended family, both old and new.

2. Verse

Philippians 4:8 (NASB)

> *"Finally, brethren, whatever is true, whatever is honorable, whatever is right, whatever is pure, whatever is lovely, whatever is of good repute, if there is any excellence and if anything worthy of praise, dwell on these things."*

Ephesians 6:11 (NASB)

> *"Put on the full armor of God, so that you will be able to stand firm against the schemes of the devil."*

3. Quote

Joseph Barth

> *"Marriage is our last, best chance to grow up."*

4. Questions

1. Which type of co-parenting relationship do you have with your children's bio parent? Perfect Pals, Cooperative Colleagues, Angry Associates, Fiery Foes, or Dissolved Duos? What improvements can be made?

   _____

   _____

   _____

   _____

   _____

   _____

   _____

2. Is your transition with your kids from one home to the other more like a POW swap or a peaceful exchange? How can you make the transition easier for your children?

   _____

   _____

   _____

   _____

   _____

   _____

   _____

3. In the name of being "a good parent," we sometimes serve our kids at the expense of our marriage.

   - On a scale of 1 to 10 (1 being the lowest), how often do you put the kids before the marriage?

     _____

   - On a scale of 1 to 10 (1 being the lowest, not putting the kids first), how often does your spouse put the kids before the marriage?

     _____

- What will you do to improve/protect the time and emotion you need for your marriage? Remember, *"If you ain't got the marriage you ain't got nothin."*

_____

_____

_____

_____

_____

_____

_____

(This is a tough balancing act. We're not putting the marriage before the kids; it's the foundation FOR the kids. It's not an and/or choice between the kids and the marriage; it's both.)

4. How do you deal with pink elephants in your family meetings? Are you avoiding them? What are they?

_____

_____

_____

_____

_____

_____

_____

5. How well are you keeping Short Accounts with your new in-laws and current extended family?

    _____

    _____

    _____

    _____

    _____

    _____

    _____

6. How well are you keeping Short Accounts with your old in-laws and previous extended family?

    _____

    _____

    _____

    _____

    _____

    _____

    _____

    _____

5. Acrostic (his, hers, and theirs): TEAM

Share from last week LAUGH

6. Add the acrostic as a brick in your wall (see pages 79)

7. Action steps

1. Plan a family meeting and share what you have learned through this study that applies to everyone.

2. Share the idea of a family acrostic using the word TEAM. Have every member work on it and come back for ice cream to share (do the acrostic on page 67).

3. Commit daily to a time of prayer with your spouse for the protection of your marriage, discernment with your kids, and wisdom for the future.

4. Share your acrostic.

5. Plan a date with your spouse with these conditions:

   • No talking about kids, money, pets, in-laws, out-laws, job, or ex's!

   • We think you deserve a rest…go take a nap!

8. Closing prayer

Right NOW, we ask for wisdom in how to deal with the right NOW! Lord, we lean upon You for a word of knowledge that will pierce the darkest of situations. We are so dependent upon You to come through for us. In all our processing of life's sorrow we know we can call upon You to deliver us. Lord, we stand convinced that You will speak to us a word of peace and clarity.

Father God, guard our marriage and family in a culture that battles against the legacy of trust and honesty. We pray that each member of the new family will enjoy freedom and knowledge of safety for a place to grieve and heal. Show us each day new ways to gently encourage one another plus wisdom to know where to give space in our relationships. We ask for a wholeness and laughter that is genuine for all to benefit from. We trust You, Jesus. Amen!

TEAM

Marked by devotion for YOUR TEAM toward a common goal

	HERS	HIS	THEIRS
T			
E			
A			
M			

"For My yoke is easy and My burden is light."

Matthew 11:30 (NASB)

TEAM: Two or more draft animals harnessed to the same vehicle or implement.

Don't forget to have

our Lord

on your TEAM, too!

Week 8

Sex and Money

Don't Fight Naked

1. Intro

Sex and money have the makings of some interesting dynamics in a remarriage relationship. When it comes to these subjects, we may have to face off with Old Tapes tied to Phantoms combined with Sneaker Waves washing over Bare Wires.

Sex in marriage is an incredible gift. As powerful as it is, it can also be easily derailed. We may have the best of intentions, then life ramps up. We need to come behind our wall to protect this part of our relationship. Your bedroom is a good thermometer as to how the rest of your relationship is going. If there are issues you are not addressing outside of your bedroom, the buck will stop there.

Who created this whole sex stuff anyway? Christ wants our relationship in the bedroom to be wonderful. It is a special gift He has given us for each other. Adjust your expectations and pray about this intimate part of your relationship, especially if you have some obstacles to overcome. Then allow the sparks to rekindle in each other's eyes. Then practice, practice, practice!

What kind of attitude do you have about money? Family of origin issues and old spending/saving patterns will play into this mindset. Trust and honesty are key players in this arena. Money can

represent strings of security, safety, control, and fear of not adequately providing. Juggling money in a remarriage will keep you on your toes. Make sure you take the time to look after your financial future, too. When it comes to money issues with adult children, good communication is the key. Keeping short accounts with your kids will deflate any growing tensions or manipulations of inheritance or other financial issues.

Don't discount the importance of the last concept of not fighting naked. We are in a battle for our marriages and our families. Don't fight naked – put on the armor of God! Read Ephesians 6:10-19 to appreciate the whole concept of putting on the armor. What we see in the physical realm is an effect of what is happening in the spiritual realm. Be sure you are aware and prepared. Pray a lot for wisdom and discernment for your marriage and family. Pray for one another. Besides not fighting naked, don't fight alone. Isolation is the enemy of restoration. Make it a point to connect with others living the stepfamily adventure.

2. Verse

Song of Solomon 7:10 (NIV)

"I belong to my lover, and his desire is for me."

Proverbs 15:16 (NIV)

"Better a little with the fear of the LORD than great wealth and turmoil."

3. Quote

Groucho Marx

"Whoever called it necking was a poor judge of anatomy."

Kim Hubbard (1868-1930)

"The safest way to double your money is to fold it over and put it in your pocket."

4. Questions

1. Because sex is a form of communication, trust and honesty must be established in the bedroom as well. What do you need to feel secure to be open and vulnerable in the sexual dimension of your relationship?

_____

_____

_____

_____

_____

_____

_____

2. How do you come behind your wall to protect this part of your relationship? ie: schedule sex so you won't be interrupted, lock the bedroom door, arrange for a get-a-way...

_____

_____

_____

_____

_____

_____

_____

3. When it comes to money, defenses can go up and the mortar in our wall gets chipped away.

  • On a scale of 1 to 10 (1 being the lowest), how comfortable are you talking about money?

_____

4. What money areas need attention (saving, budgeting, retirement, spending, etc.)?

_____

_____

_____

_____

_____

_____

5. What will the armor of God look like on a daily basis in the intricacies of our lives and remarriages? Write down a few thoughts after each one:

• Belt of truth

_____

_____

_____

• Breastplate of righteousness/integrity

_____

_____

_____

• Feet shod with the Gospel of peace

_____

_____

_____

• Shield of faith

_____

_____

_____

- Helmet of salvation

_____

_____

_____

- Sword of the Spirit (the Word of God)

_____

_____

_____

- Pray at all times

_____

_____

_____

6. What can you do to build supportive relationships to keep fellowship alive with other stepfamilies?

_____

_____

_____

_____

_____

_____

_____

_____

5. Acrostic (his and hers): create your own

Share from last week TEAM.

6. Add the acrostic as a brick in your wall (see pages 79)

7. Action steps

1. Go shopping for a new nightie.

2. Gather information to put together a better financial plan (if needed).

3. Meet another blended family in your community and do something together.

4. Share your own acrostic.

5. Plan a date with your spouse with these conditions:

   - No talking about kids, money, pets, in-laws, out-laws, job, or ex's!

   - Celebrate the growth you've experienced as a result of completing this study as a couple, emotionally, spiritually, and physically (Go pray). ☺

8. Closing prayer

Lord, we bring before You two of the most important things in our lives, our love life and money habits. We ask for understanding in how we care and cherish each other through the expression of our sexual love. We thank You for this incredible gift that is both honoring and fun! Protect us from all vices that would harm this treasured aspect of our relationship. With our money, Lord, we surrender any wrong ideas to the instruction of Your Word so that we will have wisdom in handling what You have given us the responsibility to manage. Amen!

Just be nice

to one another.

The Wall

**The Building of Your Wall for the
Protection of Your Marriage**

SAFETY

SAFETY

SAFETY

SAFETY

SAFETY

Commitment   CHRIST   Commitment

More Information

Most of these websites have a lot of links to more websites. Have fun!

- *The Smart Stepfamily* by Ron Deal
  www.successfulstepfamilies.com

- Blending a Family
  God Breathes on Blended Families by Moe and Paige Becnel
  www.blendingafamily.com

- Designing Dynamic Stepfamilies / Gordon and Carri Taylor
  www.designingdynamicstepfamilies.com

- *Blended Families* and *Raising Children in Blended Families* by Maxine Marsolini
  www.rebuildingfamilies.net

- Real Relationships with Drs. Les and Leslie Parrott
  Saving Your Second Marriage Before It Starts
  www.realrelationships.com

- Families Northwest
  www.familiesnorthwest.org

- InStep Ministries
  www.instepministries.com

- *Step Family Survival Guide* / Natalie Gillespie
  www.stepfamilysurvivalguide.com

- Blended Families
  www.blended-families.com

- *The Good Divorce* by Dr. Constance Ahrons
  www.constanceahrons.com

- Laugh Your Way to a Better Marriage
  www.laughyourway.com
  www.flagpage.com

- Bonus Families
  www.bonusfamilies.com

Meet the Stuarts

Gil and Brenda live in Vancouver, Washington. They have seven children between them, ages 18 to 29.

Gil graduated from Bethany Bible College. He currently is an insurance broker and active in the community with marriage and family issues.

Brenda was on staff as children's pastor of their church and now works with youth, marriage, and family initiatives.

The Stuarts deliver a fresh style of encouragement to this ever-growing population in society – the blended family. Willing to speak the obvious from their own stepfamily adventure, Gil and Brenda share heart to heart as they walk the walk.

They are partners with Marriage CoMission and are Prepare and Enrich certified through Life Innovations. They are also founding board members of Thriving Families of Clark County, Washington.

Vision Statement

The foundation of a successful remarriage is trust, honesty, commitment, and is Christ centered. A strong remarriage provides a safe place for the family to grow, mature, and heal.

Mission

"Restored & Remarried" is a fun, interactive, practical resource that will encourage and equip couples who are thinking about, starting out on, or who are living the stepfamily adventure.

> *If you ain't got the marriage, you ain't got nothin'.*

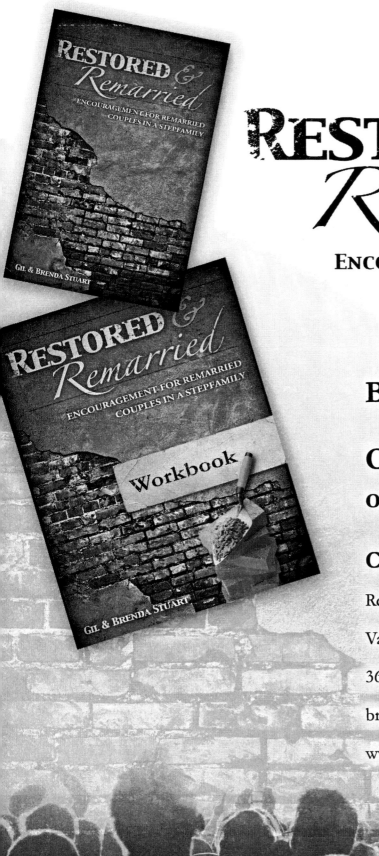

RESTORED & *Remarried*

ENCOURAGEMENT FOR REMARRIED COUPLES IN A STEPFAMILY

Book a seminar…

Order more books or workbooks…

Contact:

Restored & Remarried

Vancouver, Washington

360-604-2117

brenda@restoredandremarried.com

www.restoredandremarried.com

87